Lives
of the Artists

Marc
CHAGALL

Marc
CHAGALL

WORLD ALMANAC® LIBRARY

Please visit our web site at:
www.worldalmanaclibrary.com
For a free color catalog describing World Almanac®
Library's list of high-quality books and multimedia
programs, call 1-800-848-2928 (USA) or 1-800-387-3178
(Canada). World Almanac® Library's fax: (414) 332-3567.

Library of Congress Cataloging-in-Publication Data

Mason, Antony.
    Marc Chagall / by Antony Mason.
       p. cm. — (Lives of the artists)
    Includes index.
    ISBN 0-8368-5649-X (lib. bdg.)
    ISBN 0-8368-5654-6 (softcover)
    1. Chagall, Marc, 1887—Juvenile literature. 2. Artists—Russia
(Federation)—Biography—Juvenile literature. I. Title. II. Series.
N6999.C46M42 2004
709'.2—dc22
[B]   2004040852

This North American edition first published in 2005 by
World Almanac® Library
330 West Olive Street, Suite 100
Milwaukee, WI 53212 USA

This U.S. edition copyright © 2005 by World Almanac® Library.
Original edition copyright © 2005 McRae Books Srl.

The series "The Lives of the Artists"
was created and produced by McRae Books Srl
Borgo Santa Croce, 8 – Florence (Italy)
info@mcraebooks.com
Publishers: Anne McRae and Marco Nardi

Project Editor: Loredana Agosta
Art History consultant: Roberto Carvalho de Magalhães
Text: Antony Mason
Illustrations: Studio Stalio (Alessandro Cantucci,
Fabiano Fabbrucci, Andrea Morandi)
Graphic Design: Marco Nardi
Picture Research: Loredana Agosta
Layout: Studio Yotto
World Almanac® Library editor: JoAnn Early Macken
World Almanac® Library art direction: Tammy Gruenewald

Acknowledgments
All efforts have been made to obtain and provide compensation for the copyright
to the photos and artworks in this book in accordance with legal provisions.
Persons who may nevertheless still have claims are requested to contact the
copyright owners.
All works by Henri Matisse: ©2005 The Estate of Henri Matisse by SIAE, Rome.
All works by Marc Chagall: ©2005 The Estate of Marc Chagall by SIAE, Rome.

t=top; tl=top left; tc=top center; tr=top right; c=center; cl=center left; cr=center right;
b=bottom; bl=bottom left; bc=bottom center; br=bottom right

The publishers would like to thank the following archives who have authorized the
reproduction of the works in this book:
Artothek:35cl; The Bridgeman Art Library, London/Farabola Foto, Milan: 7t, 11r, 13b,
17b, 19cl, 21bl, 23l, 26b, 27tr, 27bl, 28b, 31bl, 33b, 35tr, 36cl, 36br, 39, 40, 42t, 42b, 45tr;
Corbis/Contrasto, Milan: 33tr, 44bl; Erich Lessing/Contrasto, Milan: 41tl; ©2003, Digital
Image, The Museum of Modern Art, New York/Scala, Florence: cover, 14t, 14bl, 15
(Mrs. Simon Guggenheim Fund), 16b (A. Rockefeller Fund), 25cl, 33tl, 45b (Acquired
through the Lillie P. Bliss Bequest. Acc.), 21tr, 25t, 32b; ©Foto Scala, Florence: 6br, 9b,
11t, 11bl, 17tc, 18cl, 19tl, 19br, 31t, 34br, 43t; ©Photo CNAC/MNAM Dist. RMN: 10b, 20cl,
22cr, 29t, 37t, 38b; ©Photo RMN – Gérard Blot: 30b, 37br; Roger-Voillet, Paris/ Fratelli
Alinari, Florence: 35bc; Rue des Archives, Paris: 7bc, 13tl, 23tr, 29bl, 37bl, 41bl; Marco
Nardi: 41br

The publishers would like to thank the following museums and institutions who
have authorized the reproduction of the works in this book: The Guggenheim, New
York: 12b; Philadelphia Museum of Art: The Louise and Walter Arensberg Collection:
24b; The Jewish Museum, New York/ Art Resource, New York: 25br

Printed in China

1 2 3 4 5 6 7 8 9 08 07 06 05 04

cover: *I and the Village*, **Museum of Modern Art, New York**

opposite: *Double Portrait with a Glass of Wine* (detail), **Musée National
    d'Art Moderne, Paris**

previous page: *Birthday*, **Museum of Modern Art, New York**

Table of Contents

Introduction

Marc Chagall (1887–1985) was Russian born, but he moved to France at the age of twenty-three and went on to became one of the best loved of the talented and innovative artists who gathered in Paris in the early twentieth century. He was a driven artist, passionate about his work, and hugely prolific — producing some ten thousand works in his lifetime. "A day without painting," he once said, "is not a real day for me." His very long life spanned the turmoil of the twentieth century, including the Russian Revolution and the two World Wars. After World War II, he enjoyed a worldwide reputation, and honors were heaped upon him.

Chagall's Life (An Overview)

1887 Born on July 7 in Vitebsk, Belarus.
1908 Trains under Léon Bakst in St. Petersburg.
1909 Meets Bella Rosenfeld and becomes engaged to her.
1911 Goes to Paris.
1914 Has a one-man show in Berlin, then is trapped in Vitebsk by World War I.
1915 Marries Bella.
1916 Their daughter Ida is born.
1919 After the Russian Revolution, Chagall sets up Academy of Arts.
1920 He designs sets, costumes, and murals for the Moscow State Yiddish Theater.
1923 He returns to Paris via Berlin.
1937 With the rising threat from Nazi Germany, he takes French citizenship.
1941 Chagall and Bella flee to the United States.
1944 Bella dies.
1946 Chagall has a son, David, with Virginia Haggard McNeil.
1948 Chagall and Virginia return to France.
1950 They move to Vence, in the South of France.
1951 Virginia leaves Chagall.
1952 He marries Valentina (Vava) Brodsky.
1964 Chagall completes his ceiling painting for the Paris Opéra.
1968 He completes his stained glass for St. Etienne Cathedral in Metz.
1985 He dies on March 28 at St.-Paul-de-Vence.

Chagall's RUSSIA

St. Petersburg

Vitebsk   Moscow

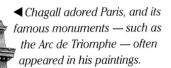

◀Chagall adored Paris, and its famous monuments — such as the Arc de Triomphe — often appeared in his paintings.

▼ Chagall was nearly ninety years old when he painted Joy (1976), one of a series featuring blocks of color, couples, and the artist.

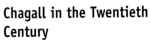

Chagall in the Twentieth Century

When Chagall arrived in Paris in 1911, the art world was in ferment. Fauvism had caused great shock and excitement in 1905, shortly to be followed by Cubism, then Futurism, Orphism, and Expressionism. After World War I came Dadaism and Suprematism. Chagall took what he wanted from these movements but resolutely stood apart from them, painting a personal, poetic vision in a way that places him in a category of his own.

Childhood Images

Early on in his career, Chagall developed a personal language of imagery that recurs in his work throughout his life. It includes farm animals, rural villagers, lone fiddlers, and flying figures. He often featured his home town of Vitebsk, even when he lived a long way from it, as if drawing comfort from his childhood memories. Perspective, or realistic sizing, rarely played any part in his composition. As a result, his painting seems to belong to a fairy tale world disconnected from consciousness — more to do with dreams, memories, and emotion than the description of reality.

▶ Peasant Life *(1925) depicts a rural scene with Russian elements, despite the fact that it was painted when Chagall was living in Paris.*

Revolutionary Times

It was not just the art world that was in turmoil in the early twentieth century. So too was Chagall's homeland, Russia. In 1917, after years of tension, the government of Russia was overthrown by revolution, and the czar was executed, paving the way for a Communist government. Although it raised hopes for a better, fairer deal for the majority of Russians, years of chaos ensued, resolved only when the Communists imposed their rule by brutal force.

▲ *A heroic Bolshevik waving the red flag of Communism is celebrated in a painting designed to promote Russian revolutionary propaganda.*

▶ *In 1963, at the age of seventy-six, Chagall undertook one of his most ambitious projects, painting a vast canvas for the ceiling of the Paris Opéra.*

More Than Just a Painter

Chagall is best known for his paintings, which certainly consumed most of his time and energy. He was also a noted theatrical designer, creating stage sets and costumes for productions from 1920 onward. In his thirties, he began to do etchings to illustrate books, quickly gaining recognition as a master of printmaking. Later in life, he learned the art of stained glass and designed spectacular windows for a number of major buildings. He also designed tapestries and mosaics and made pottery and sculpture. To each of these different modes of expression he applied his own distinctive imagery and vision, so a clear family link unites them all.

The Russian Boy

The artist who became known to the world as Marc Chagall was born with the name Moshe Segal in 1887 in the small industrial city of Vitebsk (or Vitsyebsk) in Belarus in eastern Europe. At that time, Belarus (or Belarussia) was ruled by Russia. Chagall's family was devoutly Jewish and part of a large Jewish community in Vitebsk. He was the eldest of nine children. His father worked in a warehouse dealing in herring, while his mother ran a grocery shop. It was not an artistic family. In fact, Chagall later claimed that he was eighteen when he first saw a fellow school pupil make a drawing, and from that moment, he wanted to become an artist.

► *An old postcard shows the Grand Synagogue of Vitebsk, a focal point for the city's Jewish community.*

The Jewish People in Russia

The Jews formed a distinct community in Russia, with their own customs, religious practices, and eating habits. They spoke not only Russian but also the Jewish language called Yiddish, a mixture of German, Hebrew, and Slavic. In part, their separateness was forced upon them by a long tradition of anti-Semitism. Anti-Jewish victimization and violent oppression remained a feature of European history through most of Chagall's life.

◄ *Detail of a painting titled* After the Pogrom *(1905), by Maurycy Minkowski (1881–1930).*

Growing Up in Vitebsk

Like many cities of eastern Europe at that time, Vitebsk had a large Jewish community of about forty-eight thousand people — over half the population of the city. Chagall was brought up as a Hasidic Jew with a strong tradition in folklore, poetry, music, and dance, all of which strongly colored his childhood. He went to a Jewish primary school (or cheder). Normally, because he was Jewish, he would not have been able to go to the Russian-speaking state school, but in 1900, his determined mother managed to get him a place.

▼ *The Winter Palace in St. Petersburg was the residence of the czar (the Russian emperor) and his family.*

Saint Petersburg

In 1906, at age nineteen, Chagall left Vitebsk to study art in St. Petersburg. At that time, St. Petersburg was the capital of Russia and the center of its artistic life. Because of the restrictions imposed on Jews, it required great determination for Chagall to survive there. He lived in poverty, retouching photographs, and registered as a domestic servant.

Revolutionary Ideas

St. Petersburg was a sophisticated international city. But most Russians were poor and downtrodden and ruled by a small minority of wealthy landowners and aristocrats. For several decades, various left-wing political movements had tried to bring about change, and Russia had been rocked by strikes, riots, and bombings. Just two years before Chagall reached St. Petersburg, in January 1905, a large demonstration ended in a massacre called Bloody Sunday. This event triggered a widespread revolt that nearly became a full-scale revolution.

Léon Bakst

In St. Petersburg, Chagall got a place to study art at the School of the Imperial Society for the Protection of Fine Arts. He moved to a private academy before being accepted in 1908 to join the Svanseva School, whose head was Léon Bakst (1866–1925). Bakst, an artist of great originality, was a founding member of the World of Art group, whose aim was to bring together the trends in current European art. Another member was Sergei Pavlovich Diaghilev (1872–1929), who in 1909 launched the Ballets Russes in Paris — Europe's most exciting ballet company. Bakst designed the sets and costumes.

Chagall's Early Works

Already in these early days, Chagall's highly individual style and choice of themes were beginning to emerge. Often drawing on folklore and subjects from his childhood in Vitebsk, he painted with a poetic, almost childlike style, as if inspired more by imagination than what he saw in reality. He used this style also to illustrate his newfound love for Bella Rosenfeld, whom he met in 1909. His approach to painting was a reaction against the realistic, technically polished style of the leading Russian artists of the day, such as Ilya Repin (1844–1930), but it was more in tune with new trends in art in Paris.

► *Bella, Chagall's future wife, was pictured in this portrait,* My Fiancée with Black Gloves *(1909).*

▲ *The great novelist Leo Tolstoy (1828–1910), here seen in a portrait by Ilya Repin, played a major part in shaping criticism of the Russian government.*

◄ Narcissus *(1911) was one of the productions of the Ballets Russes for which Bakst designed the costumes, winning international acclaim.*

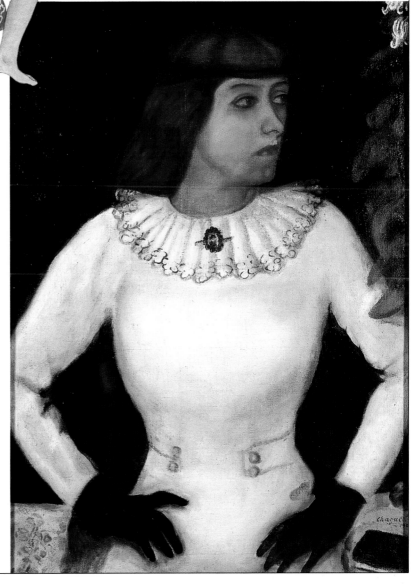

Paris Hothouse

In 1911, Chagall was able to realize a dream and travel to Paris. The trip would have been impossible without the generous financial assistance of a benefactor, Maxim Vinaver (1863–1926), a patron of the arts and a member of the Russian parliament. Paris at this time was the center of the art world, where all the most exciting trends in art were taking place. Chagall was inspired by these trends, but his imagination was still full of his Russian-Jewish background and memories of Vitebsk.

Montparnasse

For the previous forty years or so, the artistic center in Paris had been Montmartre. Artists such as Claude Monet (1840–1926) and Henri de Toulouse-Lautrec (1864–1901) had gathered there. Now the artistic focus was shifting south of the Seine River to Montparnasse, where rents were cheaper. Chagall rented and lived in a small studio in Montparnasse for the next year and a half.

▼ *Chagall's painting* The Studio *(1910) echoes van Gogh's efforts to portray his own personal world.*

▶ *Montparnasse attracted numerous artists, such as the sculptor Émile-Antoine Bourdelle (1861–1929), who created this* Hercules the Archer *(1909).*

The Poet

Despite a small income from Vinaver, Chagall was very poor — so poor that he had to paint on canvases made from old curtains. He worked by night and spent the days at art academies or visiting galleries, where he came across the work of contemporary and recent artists, such as Vincent van Gogh (1853–90). Speaking little French, lonely, impoverished, driven by his art — but also charismatic, good-looking, and thrilled to be in Paris — Chagall was nicknamed "The Poet."

Fauvism

One of the first and most important art movements of the twentieth century was Fauvism. One of its leaders was Henri Matisse (1869–1954), who took Impressionism and Post-Impressionism one step further by filling his paintings with bright and unrealistic colors. He also created unconventional compositions based on imagination. When Fauvism was launched in Paris in 1905, it caused excitement, shock, and outrage. The movement lasted only a couple of years but had a major impact.

▲ *By the time Chagall arrived in Paris, the leader of Fauvism, Henri Matisse, had moved on to a slightly more controlled style, as seen in* The Dance *(1910), a subject that fascinated him.*

▼ *Portrait of Ambroise Vollard (1910) by Picasso. Cubism was applied to this portrait of the famous art dealer.*

Cubism

The next big art movement was Cubism, which began in 1907 and remained the most important trend until 1914. It was led by Pablo Picasso (1881–1973), a Spanish artist living in Paris, and the French painter Georges Braque (1882–1963). Picasso and Braque were inspired by the success of Fauvism to invent a new way of representing the visual world. They did this by breaking up compositions into geometric shapes (such as cubes), and showing them as if seen from different angles at once. Along with Braque, Picasso also started using collage and sculpture, introduced unusual materials into his work, and generally brought a new freedom to art. The result shocked many members of the public but inspired countless young artists, including Chagall.

▼ *Much had changed in the art world since van Gogh painted* The Bedroom *(1888), but his work remained an inspiration to many artists.*

Artists and Poets

1912 He exhibits three paintings, including *To Russia, to Donkeys, and to the Others*, at the Salon des Indépendants, the important if controversial annual showcase for new art. He also exhibits three paintings at the Salon d'Automne, another annual exhibition of modern art. He meets the art dealer and publisher Herwarth Walden. Guillaume Apollinaire identifies a new art movement called Orphism.

1913 Chagall meets Guillaume Apollinaire. He exhibits two paintings at the Salon des Indépendants.

1914 He exhibits three paintings at the Salon des Indépendants.

The feverish artistic atmosphere in Paris produced a succession of new and inventive art movements. The mood excited Chagall and encouraged him to experiment and to become ever more daring in his work. After moving to the artists' colony called La Ruche, he received plenty of encouragement from other artists and poets — notably the writer and art critic Guillaume Apollinaire, a great champion of modern art since the days of Fauvism. His closest friend, however, was a French poet and writer of Swiss origin, Blaise Cendrars (1887–1961), a fellow resident at La Ruche.

◀ *The verve of Paris's artists and designers was reflected in the new entrances to the Métro stations in Art Nouveau style by Hector Guimard (1867–1942).*

My Second Vitebsk

Through personal contacts and his visits to galleries and exhibitions, Chagall now knew the work of numerous artists, both contemporary and from the past. He absorbed their lessons, but from them he developed a way of painting that was entirely his own, adapted to his own vision of the world — part real, part imagined. This personalized style stayed with him for the rest of his life. Many observers say that the work Chagall did in Paris at this time ranks among the best of his career. He acknowledged his debt to Paris, calling it "my second Vitebsk."

▶ *The recognizable world (including the Eiffel Tower) merges with the inner world of Chagall's imagination in* Paris through the Window *(1913), painted at La Ruche.*

La Ruche

In the winter of 1911, Chagall moved to La Ruche in the Vaugirard quarter of Paris, a little to the west of Montparnasse. This was an artists' colony containing one hundred forty studios, built in 1900 to accommodate artists and writers from all over the world at low cost. Although still impoverished, Chagall was able to afford a large, well-lit studio on the top floor. Among the artists, there were a number who later achieved international fame. They included Amedeo Modigliani (1884–1920), an Italian who had arrived in Paris in 1906, and the French artist Fernand Léger (1881–1955), a painter inspired by Cubism and Futurism. The Russian painter Chaim Soutine (1894–1943), who worked in the new Expressionist style, arrived in 1913.

◄ *The name "La Ruche" means "the beehive" — an apt description of both how it looked and the busy activity inside.*

◄ *"La Colombe" (the Dove), a poem-picture by Guillaume Apollinaire, shows his innovative approach to presentation.*

▼ *The onion-domed church in* To Russia, to Donkeys and to the Others *(1911–12) clearly links the painting to Chagall's homeland.*

Guillaume Apollinaire

One of the most significant figures of the Paris art scene was the French writer and poet Guillaume Apollinaire (1880–1918), who was a friend of many of the key artists of the day, including Chagall. Inspired by Cubism, which included some written words in collages, Apollinaire sought ways to combine words with visual ideas, and he created poem pictures that he called Calligrammes. He believed this fusion of words and image produced a strange kind of supernatural effect — an effect that he also saw in Chagall's work.

Memories of Russia

Despite his fascination and love for Paris, Chagall remained obsessed by recollections of his childhood in Vitebsk, and many of the subject matters of his works were drawn entirely from his memory and imagination. *To Russia, to Donkeys and to the Others* appears to tell some kind of Russian folktale, but the obscure title, suggested by Blaise Cendrars, in fact refers to a 1912 art exhibition in Moscow called *The Donkey's Tail*.

Artists and Poets

Robert Delaunay and Orphism

Another new direction in art was taken in about 1912 by a movement named Orphism by Guillaume Apollinaire. It centered on work by artists such as the French painter Robert Delaunay (1885–1941) and Fernand Léger, who were inspired by Cubism but found its approach too austere and scientific. Instead, they injected color into their paintings and likened their work to music. Delaunay was an early pioneer in what became known as abstract art — compositions of colors and shapes without any reference at all to the visual or real world. His work was a major inspiration to German artists working in the style called Expressionism.

▶ Simultaneous Contrasts: Sun and Moon *(1912–13), by Robert Delaunay, is an experiment in pure color but still bears marks of Cubist inspiration.*

◀ *Futurism made front-page news in the French newspaper* Le Figaro, *which also printed the* Futurist Manifesto, *a statement of the movement's intentions.*

▼ *A detail from* I and the Village *(1911) demonstrates Chagall's approach to painting in which "logic and illustration have no importance."*

Futurism

In 1909, a new art movement was founded by the Italian poet Filippo Tommaso Marinetti (1876–1944) and relaunched with great flourish with an exhibition in Paris in 1912. The Futurists declared noisily that they wanted to sweep aside all old traditions of art to create a new and vibrant kind of art that was in tune with the modern age of machines and speed. The main artists — such as Umberto Boccioni (1882–1916) and Giacomo Balla (1871–1958) — were also Italian, but their ideas inspired many French artists, including Delaunay.

I and the Village

It is possible to detect ways in which Chagall was affected by other artists of the day. There are echoes of Cubism and of Delaunay's colors in *I and the Village*. But the themes emerging in his paintings — the floating figures, animals, Russian buildings, characters from folklore, scenes from everyday life, the lone violinist — give Chagall's paintings a mysterious and whimsical charm that is quite his own. When asked to explain his work, Chagall replied, "I don't understand them myself. They are not literature. They are only pictorial arrangements, which obsess me."

▼ I and the Village *(1911) uses a carefully constructed mosaic of superimposed images to evoke a fragmented narrative rather like a dream.*

Berlin and War

1914 In May, Chagall travels to Berlin to arrange his first one-man exhibition at Der Sturm Gallery. In June, the exhibition opens and is critically acclaimed. On June 15, he travels on to Russia, leaving all his work in Berlin. He is reunited with Bella in Vitebsk. On June 28, Archduke Franz Ferdinand of Austria is assassinated. In August, Germany declares war on Russia and then France. Chagall is trapped in Vitebsk.

Bella Rosenfeld was rarely out of Chagall's mind when he was in Paris, and he longed to see her again. In 1914, prompted by Guillaume Apollinaire, the German art dealer Herwarth Walden offered to give Chagall an exhibition at his gallery in Berlin. For the twenty-six-year-old Chagall, it was an opportunity not to be missed: it was his first one-man show, and he could travel on from there to Vitebsk. He hoped to return to Paris after three months, but in August 1914, World War I broke out. Subsequent political events kept Chagall in Russia for the next eight years.

◀ *The cover of an edition of the weekly magazine* Der Sturm *draws the eye with a typically dynamic illustration.*

▼ *Kandinsky's* Panel for Edwin R. Campbell No. 2 *(1914) is typical of his nonobjective art. The title underlines the fact that it bears no link to the visual world.*

▲ *The Brandenburg Gate in Berlin, built as a triumphal arch in 1791, was a symbol of German national pride.*

On Display in Berlin

The gallery of Herwarth Walden (1878–1941) in Berlin was no ordinary gallery: it was Der Sturm (meaning "the storm" in German), a place where — since its opening in 1912 — the work of many avant-garde artists of the day were shown. Walden's magazine, also called *Der Sturm*, was a leading arts journal and the voice of the German Expressionists. Chagall showed 150 works on paper and forty paintings, including *To Russia, to Donkeys and to the Others* and *I and the Village*, which caused a sensation.

Nonobjective Art

The German Expressionists were a loose group of artists pursuing a wide variety of styles and objectives. What united them was a desire to inject emotion, imagination, and color in their work, taking Fauvism to the next stage. Among them was the Russian-born artist Wassily Kandinsky (1866–1944), who was closely associated with Der Sturm. Returning to his studio in Munich one night in 1910, Kandinsky found one of his paintings the wrong way up and loved it. This led him to start painting nonobjective art, another term for abstract art. Kandinsky went on to form part of the German group of Expressionists called Der Blaue Reiter (The Blue Rider).

The Outbreak of War

The rivalry between the great imperial powers — France, Britain, and Russia versus Germany, Austria-Hungary, and Turkey — placed Europe under great strain for at least a decade. In 1914, Archduke Franz Ferdinand (1863–1914), heir to the throne of Austria-Hungary, was assassinated in Sarajevo. This brought into play pledges of mutual support among the alliances: Germany declared war on Russia and then France. Britain declared war on Germany. The result was World War I, which lasted until 1918.

◀ *Industrial Europe produced a new breed of devastating heavy guns, such as the type of German howitzer known as "Big Bertha."*

▲ *Soldier at Rest (1911) by Mikhail Larionov seems to anticipate the war that erupted three years later.*

▼ *Chagall's Over Vitebsk (1914) is a kind of visual pun. In Yiddish, a wanderer is someone who "walks over the town."*

Back in Vitebsk

With the outbreak of war, Chagall was stuck in Vitebsk, a city he now found rather dull. Despite his absence of four years, he was quickly able to rekindle his close relationship with Bella, who was back from her acting studies in Moscow under the great theater director Konstantin Stanislavsky (1863–1938). Chagall continued to work, painting mainly local scenes, family, and friends. Many of these paintings were later exhibited in Moscow alongside work by the avant-garde Jack of Diamonds group, which was associated with Russia's leading abstract artist, Mikhail Larionov (1881–1964).

The Home Front

1915 Paintings by Chagall are included in the Salon exhibition in Moscow. In July, he marries Bella in Vitebsk. He goes to Petrograd to work in the Ministry of War Economy. There he begins to write his autobiography *My Life*.
1916 Bella gives birth to a daughter, Ida. Chagall's paintings are included in the Jack of Diamonds exhibition in Moscow. The detested holy man Grigory Yefimovich Rasputin (c. 1872–1916), adviser to the czar's wife, is murdered in Petrograd.

In July 1915, Chagall and Bella were married. On the one hand, he was thrilled; on the other, the world picture was gloomy. The war seemed to be coming ever closer, threatening their future. Chagall managed to avoid military service, but only by taking a job as a clerk in the Ministry of War Economy in St. Petersburg — or Petrograd, as it had now been renamed. Separated from Bella, he maintained his artistic life through contacts with some of the leading Russian writers and exhibiting paintings in Moscow. Russian art collectors were beginning to take serious interest in his work.

▼ Chagall's Red Jew *(1915)* *was a direct response to the arrival of Jewish refugees in Vitebsk.*

The Arrival of Refugees

Russian troops clashed with the Germans along a front that sliced through eastern Europe. The war displaced hundreds of thousands of people, who fled eastward. The Jews were victims of another kind: distrusted and suspected of spying, they suffered repeated pogroms in Russia. More than two hundred thousand Jews were evicted from the war zone in Lithuania in May 1915. Many of them sought refuge in Vitebsk. Their pathetic plight deeply affected Chagall and reinforced his feelings for his Jewish heritage.

▲ *Vladimir Mayakovsky took an active role in the Russian Futurist movement.*

Russian Poets

Chagall hated his work in Petrograd and traveled as often as he could to visit Bella. Contact with a number of Russian poets and writers compensated for his life in Petrograd. His associates included the poet Aleksandr Blok (1880–1921), who wrote mystical Symbolist work, the poet and later novelist Boris Pasternak (1890–1960), and the young poet and dramatist Vladimir Mayakovsky (1893–1930).

◀ *Many soldiers of World War I were blinded by gas.*

The War Front

The war was going badly for Russia. It was badly fought and badly managed. The Russian army lost ground against Germany so that by the beginning of 1917, the front was only 93 miles (150 km) from Vitebsk. The city was swelled with some forty thousand soldiers, some heading for the front, some returning with their wounds. The czar, who in 1915 appointed himself supreme commander of the Russian army, was held personally responsible for the progress of the war — and for the chaos and food shortages that were suffered by the civilians.

▼ *A detail from Chagall's* Double Portrait with a Glass of Wine *shows the landscape and monastery of Vitebsk as if dwarfed by the joyous emotion of the couple.*

▶ Double Portrait with a Glass of Wine *(1917–18) shows Chagall riding on the shoulders of Bella and Ida descending like an angel.*

▲ Baby's Bath *(1916) shows Chagall's delight in the everyday rituals of parenthood.*

The Birth of Ida

Chagall and Bella were thrilled by the birth of their daughter Ida in May 1916. She was the only child Chagall and Bella had. The family always remained a close and tight-knit unit of three. Chagall made a number of drawings and paintings of Bella with baby Ida that were affectionate images of tenderness.

Marrying Bella

Chagall had been engaged to Bella Rosenfeld for about six years before they were finally married. Bella's family was not happy with the match. The Rosenfelds were fairly wealthy merchants who lived in some style in Vitebsk. Chagall's family was poor by comparison; his father worked as a fishmonger's assistant. Furthermore, Chagall's future as an artist looked precarious. Nonetheless, they could not fault the couple's devotion to each other. They were married in July 1915 by a rabbi in a Jewish ceremony. Chagall showed his deep love for Bella by including her in countless paintings and drawings and often depicted the two of them as a couple floating above the ground, as if physically transported by their love.

Revolution

1917 In February, riots erupt in Petrograd over food shortages. The revolt spreads, and in March, the czar abdicates. In October, Communists take power in the Russian Revolution.
1918 Russia withdraws from World War I. The capital is transferred from Petrograd to Moscow. Chagall, Bella, and Ida return to Vitebsk. At the First State Exhibition of Revolutionary Art at the Winter Palace in Petrograd, Chagall's work is given two rooms, a special honor. Chagall sets up the Academy of Arts in Vitebsk, which is inaugurated on January 28. Shortly afterward, he resigns.
1920 Chagall leaves Vitebsk for Moscow.

When the Russian Revolution erupted in October 1917, Chagall found himself in a position of influence. He was broadly in sympathy with the revolutionaries, and the new government needed people to run the ministries. As a leading avant-garde artist, he was invited to be Director of Fine Art in the Ministry of Culture in Petrograd; his friend, the poet Mayakovsky, was to be Director of Poetry. But Bella persuaded Chagall not to become involved in politics and to return to Vitebsk instead. Nonetheless, he threw himself into the task of establishing a new art school, and he was appointed Commissar for the Fine Arts for Vitebsk to carry out the task.

◀ *An illustration from* The Jewish Worker, *a newspaper of Austria and Poland, shows a heroic blacksmith hammering a Star of David, the Jewish emblem.*

A New Hope for a Better Future

The Russian Revolution was a popular revolt supported by a broad cross-section of society, from the peasants and industrial laborers to the middle classes. It held out the prospect of a fairer society with a more even distribution of the nation's wealth. Jews took a prominent part in the Revolution, and among the Jewish population as a whole there was — for a short while — some hope of equal rights and an end to their oppression. But in fact the pogroms continued, and the country was soon plunged into a long and bitter civil war that lasted until 1921.

◀ *The Cemetery Gates (1917) underlines Chagall's bond with his Jewish background. Despite the subject, the theme is hope and resurrection.*

The Russian Revolution

In 1917, long-term resentments, opposition to World War I, and food shortages combined to create the Russian Revolution, which turned Russia into a Communist state. In February, the Mensheviks led a revolt in Petrograd that overthrew the government and dethroned the czar. They hoped to establish a democratic republic along the lines of other European countries. In October, soldiers mutinied, and Communist revolutionaries called Bolsheviks, led by Vladimir Ilich Lenin (1870–1924), overthrew the Provisional Government.

▶ *Malevich's* Suprematist Composition: Airplane Flying *(1915) shows the radically austere nature of his art, which was quite different from Chagall's.*

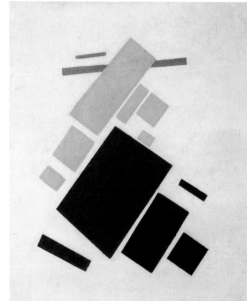

◀ *Lenin was portrayed as a heroic revolutionary leader, but his rule soon became an oppressive dictatorship.*

▶ *Nicholas II (1895–1917) was the last of the Romanov czars, who had ruled Russia for three hundred years. He was executed in 1918.*

The Vitebsk Academy

Chagall wanted to make his Academy of Arts in Vitebsk into one of the leading art schools in Russia. To achieve this, he invited some of the most exciting Russian artists of the day to teach there. They included the painter and designer El Lissitzky (1890–1941) and also Kasimir Malevich (1878–1935), the founder of a new art movement called Suprematism. Limiting himself to geometric shapes and a narrow range of colors, Malevich created the most austere abstract art the world had yet seen. He was also strident and ambitious, and he soon quarreled with Chagall.

A Question of Politics

To show his support for the Revolution, Chagall organized the artists and craftsmen of Vitebsk to make elaborate street decorations for celebrations to mark the first anniversary of the Revolution. At the school, he found it difficult to come to terms with the political intrusion of the government. The authorities supported the kind of revolutionary art represented by Malevich and Suprematism and the equally uncompromising Constructivism, which championed industrial-style abstract art. Chagall lost the contest, and in 1919, while he was away on one of his frequent trips to Moscow, Malevich took over the school and renamed it the Suprematist Academy. Feeling deeply betrayed, Chagall resigned, and in 1920, he, Bella, and Ida left Vitebsk for Moscow.

◀ War on the Palaces *(1918). Chagall designed banners to celebrate the anniversary of the Revolution, but the authorities were not enthusiastic about his folk art imagery.*

Moscow

1920 Chagall becomes involved in theater design in Moscow. He paints murals for the Moscow State Yiddish Theater — the first of his large-scale mural projects.

1921 The Moscow State Yiddish Theater opens on January 1 with three plays by Sholom Aleichem with costumes and sets designed by Chagall. His work runs into official criticism, and the theater suffers financial crisis. He moves outside Moscow to Malakhovka, where he teaches children at an orphanage. His work on his autobiography, *My Life*, begins in earnest.

Chagall and Bella had always been interested in theater. When Chagall became involved in set and costume design in Moscow, both welcomed the change. Chagall was also invited to work for the new State Yiddish Theater Company. He threw himself into this project and won acclaim for his work. But the political and economic situation in postrevolutionary Russia was deteriorating. Out of tune with official taste, Chagall faced poverty and rejection and took up teaching at an orphanage. Once championed as a leading artist of the new Russia, he now felt isolated and unappreciated.

Moscow, the New Capital

Moscow was the old capital of Russia. It lost this role in 1712 when Czar Peter the Great (1672–1725) moved the capital to his brand-new and spectacular city of St. Petersburg, which gave him better access to Europe. The Communist revolutionaries moved the capital back to Moscow in 1918, partly because it was more centrally located and partly because of St. Petersburg's links to the royal family. Moscow became the center of the Russian art world.

◄ *Stalin came from humble origins to take a leading role in the Bolshevik movement and the Revolution. He ruled the Soviet Union with an iron fist until his death in 1953.*

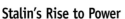
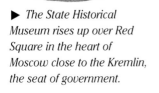

▶ *The State Historical Museum rises up over Red Square in the heart of Moscow close to the Kremlin, the seat of government.*

Stalin's Rise to Power

During Chagall's time in Moscow, Lenin remained the leader of Russia. The Communist government was fighting a civil war and felt under constant threat from counterrevolutionaries. Lenin's response was to crush all opposition brutally, but in 1922 he suffered two strokes, which left him partially paralyzed. This gave the general secretary of the Communist Party, Joseph Stalin (1879–1953), the opportunity to augment the government's dictatorial powers. Stalin, after a power struggle with Leon Trotsky (1879–1940), took over the leadership of Russia (renamed the Soviet Union) on Lenin's death in 1924.

▶ *Leon Trotsky, an intellectual of Jewish origin, was one of the leaders of the 1917 Revolution. He was considered the natural successor to Lenin but was usurped by Stalin and forced into exile in 1929.*

▲ *Chagall designed the set and costumes for a one-act play in Yiddish called* The Agents, *by Sholom Aleichem (1859–1916), which was performed at the opening of the Moscow State Yiddish Theater in 1921.*

▼ *Chagall's murals for the Moscow State Yiddish Theater were called an* Introduction to the Jewish Theater *(1920), with one huge painting and a number of smaller panels. This is the design for the panel called* Music.

▶ *Chagall, aged thirty-four, receives the rapt attention of his pupils at the Malakhovka War Orphan Colony.*

The Theater

In the feverish atmosphere of postrevolutionary Russia, the theater became a vibrant forum for new ideas. Chagall was particularly attracted to the new Moscow State Yiddish Theater, founded in 1919, which became one of the most important centers in Moscow for the promotion of Jewish culture. In 1920, he was invited to decorate the auditorium of the theater. He turned it into a magical space that became known as "Chagall's Box." Although the public and the actors loved his murals and set designs, his work was criticized by other artists, notably Malevich, but also Kandinsky, now living in Moscow, and Aleksandr Rodchenko (1891–1956), a leading Constructivist. Meanwhile, his set designs for a new play at the celebrated Moscow Art Theater — directed by Konstantin Stanislavsky — were also turned down.

Teaching Children

During 1921, the Moscow State Yiddish Theater ran into financial difficulties. Chagall moved with his family to cheaper accommodations in Malakhovka, a provincial town near Moscow, where he was offered the job of teaching at an orphanage for children who had lost their parents in the war. He turned out to be a good teacher and took pleasure in the enthusiastic and uncomplicated responses of the children. But he had become disillusioned. Essentially, his painting was out of keeping with trends of Revolutionary Russia — and so too, from 1922, was the work of the Suprematists and Constructivists. Under Stalin, the favored kind of art was more blatantly realistic and designed principally to provide uplifting propaganda for the government.

Abandoning Russia

1922 Chagall decides to leave Russia for good. He returns first to Moscow, where he resumes work on his autobiography, *My Life*. In May, he travels to Lithuania, where he has an exhibition. Then he continues to Berlin, where, during the summer, he is joined by Bella and Ida. He begins his career as a printmaker. He fails to recover the paintings left in Berlin in 1914.

1923 A book on Chagall is published in Germany, augmenting his international reputation. In August, Chagall, Bella, and Ida leave Berlin for Paris.

During 1922, it became clear to Chagall that his future did not lie in Russia. Under the Communist regime, he needed government approval for his work to survive as an active artist, but his paintings were no longer appreciated. The situation looked hopeless. He recalled his dream of 1914 to return to Paris and decided that he had to move. A friend and poet called Ludwig Rubiner (1881–1920) had written from Berlin some time before to say that Chagall was famous there. Chagall decided first to stop off in Berlin, hoping to recover his paintings from the 1914 exhibition.

Back in Germany

Germany had signed an armistice at the end of World War I in 1918; it had not surrendered. Nonetheless, at the Treaty of Versailles of 1919, it was forced to pay huge war reparations. This forced Germany into a prolonged state of poverty and stirred up fervent, sometimes violent, political debate between Democrats, Communists, and right-wing parties. The atmosphere in Berlin was feverish but also exciting, which affected the art world. Georg Grosz (1893–1959) and Otto Dix (1891–1969) were among a group of controversial, politically engaged painters.

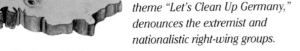

▲ *A Democratic Party poster, with the theme "Let's Clean Up Germany," denounces the extremist and nationalistic right-wing groups.*

Chagall's Lost Works

When Chagall left Berlin in 1914, he placed his forty paintings and 160 gouaches — his best work from his Paris years — in the hands of gallery owner Herwarth Walden for safekeeping. During Chagall's eight years in Russia, Walden busily promoted Chagall's work, and — unbeknown to Chagall — sold many of the paintings. When Chagall returned to Berlin, he tried to reclaim the paintings — or at least some money. Walden assured Chagall that he had placed the money owed to him safely with a lawyer. But the value of money had decreased dramatically, making Chagall's share virtually worthless. Walden gave Chagall no help in trying to recover the paintings, and the dispute resulted in a bitter court case. Chagall felt that he had been robbed not only of his money but his artistic past. In the end, in 1926, he won back just three of the paintings and ten gouaches. He spent many years making new versions of the lost paintings.

▶ Half Past Three (the Poet), *which Chagall had painted in Paris in 1911, was one of the few missing works that Chagall managed to recover.*

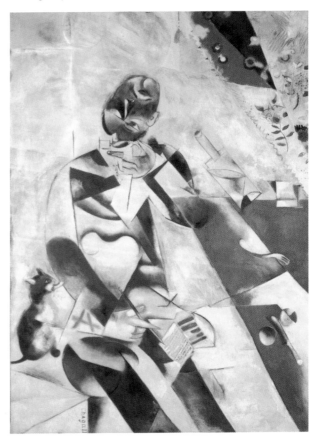

Dadaism: Anti-Art

A new and deliberately shocking art trend called Dadaism emerged in Switzerland during World War I and spread after 1918 to various cities, such as Berlin, Paris, Barcelona, and New York. It made fun of traditional ideas about art. Artists, writers, and musicians created works and performances which — so the participants claimed — had no meaning at all. Poets spouted gibberish and rude words; exhibitions were held in which visitors were encouraged to destroy the exhibits. Painting and sculptures were made from whatever materials the artists wanted to throw together. Participants included Marcel Duchamp (1887–1968), a French artist living in New York, and the German Max Ernst (1891–1976). Dadaism was contradictory and anarchic — and to many observers of the art world, infuriating. But it caused people to think again about the very nature of art.

▶ *In* The Hat Makes the Man *(1920), Max Ernst used collage to present an absurd visual image of a play on words.*

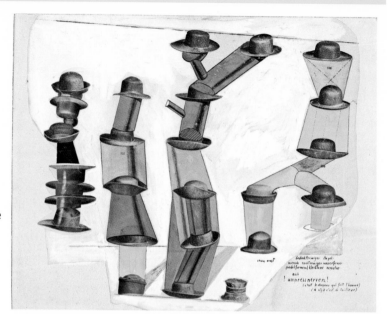

▶ Woman Combing her Hair *(1915) is typical of the radical, Cubist-inspired sculpture of Alexander Archipenko, whom Chagall met again in Berlin.*

Émigrés in Berlin

Berlin in the postwar period was full of artists, musicians, writers, and actors from all over the world. Some were refugees — including a large number of Russians who had fled the Communist regime. Others were simply attracted by the vibrant atmosphere. They included the Russian sculptor Alexander Archipenko (1887–1964), who had lived in La Ruche in Paris when Chagall was there, had exhibited in Der Sturm Gallery in 1913, and now taught in Berlin. Kandinsky was also in Berlin.

▶ House at Vitebsk *(1922) was one of twenty etchings that Chagall made to illustrate* My Life.

My Life

For several years, Chagall had been working intermittently on his autobiography, written originally in Russian and called simply *My Life*. It was perhaps odd for a man still in his thirties to be writing an autobiography, but this was not a conventional life story. It was, rather, a book of poetic reminiscences accompanied by simple illustrations, and it tells us much about Chagall's imagination and the sources of his inspiration. In Berlin, Chagall learned the art of printmaking. He used drypoint and etching to create a series of illustrations that were partly used to illustrate *My Life*, which was published in Paris in 1931. This marked the beginning of his long and distinguished career as a printmaker.

Printmaker

Another major disappointment awaited Chagall when he returned to Paris. Some 150 paintings that he had left behind at La Ruche had disappeared: a caretaker had discarded them as worthless. His friend, the poet Blaise Cendrars, may also have sold some of them, believing that Chagall had died in the war. As a result, Chagall would have nothing more to do with him. With so many of his early paintings now gone, Chagall set about making replicas of them, a task that occupied much of the next three years. But another line of art now absorbed him. In 1923, the art dealer Ambroise Vollard launched Chagall into a new career in book illustration.

◀ *Gogol was one of the greatest Russian writers of the nineteenth century, a novelist and dramatist noted for his striking mixture of humor, fantasy, and horror.*

Ambroise Vollard

One of the central figures in the Paris art world was the gallery owner, art dealer, and publisher Ambroise Vollard (1865–1939). His distinguished career went back thirty years to when he gave Paul Cézanne (1839–1906) his first major exhibition. He represented the Impressionist Pierre-Auguste Renoir (1841–1919) and the Post-Impressionist Paul Gauguin (1848–1903) and helped to promote the careers of both Picasso and Matisse. The confidence that Vollard now placed in Chagall was a great honor.

Dead Souls

Nikolai Gogol (1809–52) wrote *Dead Souls*, a story about a rogue, in 1842. The plight of Russia was very much in the news in the 1920s, and it seemed appropriate to Vollard — at Chagall's suggestion — to publish a version of the book illustrated by a Russian artist. It took Chagall three years to complete about one hundred full-page etchings. They were not actually published until 1948.

▶ Playing Cards *(1923), a plate from* Dead Souls, *shows the originality, verve, and natural talent that Chagall brought to etching — a skill that he had only recently acquired.*

Fables

The French writer Jean de la Fontaine (1621–95) was famous for compiling a large collection of fables — amusing moral tales, usually involving animals. Eternally popular, they rank among the great classics of French literature. So Vollard was taking a risk when, in 1925, he asked Chagall, a Russian, to illustrate them. For this project, Chagall was to work in color, producing preparatory gouaches that would be converted into printing plates. This process proved difficult, and Chagall ended up making the plates himself using both etching and hand-coloring. He worked on the *Fables* for six years, from 1925 to 1931.

▶ Lion and Rat *(c. 1926) was one of the typically energetic gouaches that Chagall made to illustrate La Fontaine's* Fables *for Vollard.*

Surrealism

The big new art movement was Surrealism, which was founded in Paris in 1924 by the poet André Breton (1896–1966). It evolved out of Dadaism, but in fact the word "surrealist" had been coined in 1917 by Guillaume Apollinaire, who — much to Chagall's distress — had died from Spanish flu and war wounds in 1918. Apollinaire was referring to a notion that poetry and painting could portray a world "above reality," the curious and dreamlike realm of the unconscious mind. Artists involved in the Surrealist movement included Max Ernst, the Belgian René Magritte (1898–1967), and the Spaniard Salvador Dali (1904–89). They held Chagall in high esteem, claiming him to be a forerunner of the movement, but he did not join them.

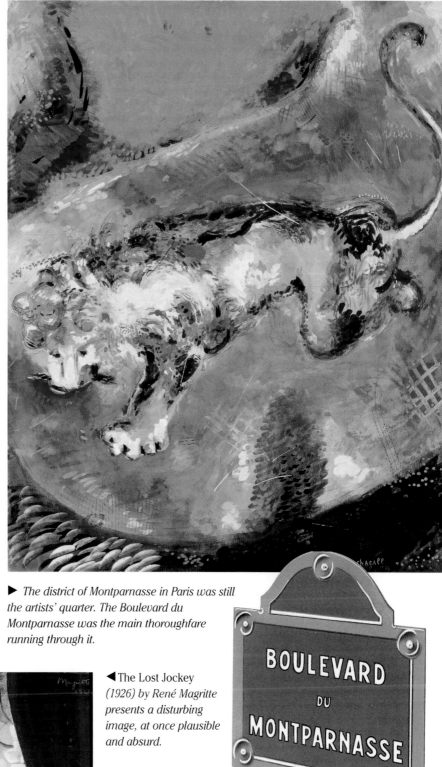

▶ *The district of Montparnasse in Paris was still the artists' quarter. The Boulevard du Montparnasse was the main thoroughfare running through it.*

◀ The Lost Jockey *(1926) by René Magritte presents a disturbing image, at once plausible and absurd.*

The School of Paris

Chagall was thrilled to be back in Paris. His joy shines through the colors in his paintings of this period. He had a wide circle of friends and acquaintances, and now that he was a successful artist, he could afford to live in some comfort. A set of foreign painters associated with Paris at this time has been loosely grouped under the title The School of Paris. They included Chaim Soutine, the Japanese painter Tsuguji Fugita (1886–1968), Amedeo Modigliani, and Chagall.

1929 The Chagalls move to the Villa Montmorency in Auteuil, in the west of Paris.
1931 *My Life* is published for the first time (as *Ma Vie*).
1933 Chagall has a large retrospective exhibition in Basel, Switzerland. Hitler comes to power in Germany on the back of anti-Jewish rabble-rousing.
1934 Ida, aged eighteen, marries Michel Gorday, a lawyer.

Painter, Printmaker, and Traveler

During the late 1920s and the 1930s, Chagall started to enjoy the comforts of success. His work was widely sought after by collectors and now fetched good prices. He at last had some financial security and was able to travel widely, both within France and abroad. He went to Palestine, to the Netherlands and England for exhibitions of his work, and to Poland as the guest of honor at the opening of a Jewish institute. He visited galleries wherever he went, studying the works of Old Masters in Amsterdam, Madrid, and Venice.

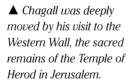

▲ *Chagall was deeply moved by his visit to the Western Wall, the sacred remains of the Temple of Herod in Jerusalem.*

A Visit to Palestine

In 1930, Vollard asked Chagall to undertake his most ambitious commission yet: to illustrate the Old Testament of the Bible with 105 plates. Chagall was delighted; the Bible had long been a profound source of inspiration to him. The following year, he was invited by the mayor of Tel Aviv to visit Palestine, and he spent three months there with Bella and Ida. He used this trip to do research and to experience for himself the places where the origins of his own Jewish identity lay.

◄ The Window on the Ile de Bréhat *(1924) is a view out onto the landscape of an island off the north coast of Brittany where Chagall spent a happy family holiday.*

Views of France

From about 1924, Chagall had begun to travel widely around France, visiting the Mediterranean, Brittany, the Alps, and the Pyrenees. In 1926, he made his first visit to the Côte d'Azur in southeastern France. He was immediately struck by the light and the landscape of this part of the Mediterranean coast. Art was often on the agenda in these trips — sketching, painting, and visiting fellow artists. In 1927, for example, he traveled with his good friend Robert Delaunay to Banyuls-sur-Mer to visit the sculptor Aristide Maillol (1861–1944).

New Freedoms

During this period, Chagall's painting became more relaxed and free. He abandoned many of the fragmented geometric forms and hard edges of his earlier work and used more painterly dabs and touches. He allowed color rather than lines to create the shapes. His subject matter included many of his old fixations — floating couples, farm animals, landmark buildings, Vitebsk — but now he also painted pure landscapes. The colors, the flowers, and the impression of contentment seem to reflect the sense of ease and pleasure in his own life.

◀ *Full of personal poetic imagery,* The Bride and Groom with Eiffel Tower *(1928) shows Chagall's new, softer style.*

André Malraux

Chagall had met the French writer André Malraux (1901–76) in 1924. Man of action, traveler, art historian, and novelist, Malraux was a keen observer of both the art world and the political world. Chagall and Malraux became close friends, and after 1958 — when he had served for ten years as Minister of Cultural Affairs — Malraux came to play a significant role in Chagall's career.

The Circus

Chagall had always been fascinated by the circus — like his paintings, a world of performing animals and acrobats defying gravity. In 1927, Vollard invited Chagall, Bella, and Ida, then eleven years old, to the Cirque d'Hiver (Winter Circus) in Paris. Chagall was thrilled and returned several times. He was easily persuaded by Vollard to paint a set of gouaches on the theme of the circus, a series of nineteen pieces called the *Cirque Vollard*. They were intended as preliminary work for a set of lithograph prints, but events prevented these being made for another twenty years.

▶ *André Malraux established his reputation with his novel* La Condition Humaine *(1933), for which he won the prestigious Prix Goncourt.*

◀*Vollard had a box at Cirque d'Hiver in Paris, built in 1852 and still one of the world's most celebrated circus venues.*

The Gathering Gloom

As the 1930s progressed, the rise of the Nazis in Germany spread an increasing sense of gloom across Europe. The Jews, above all, had reason to fear the Nazis: Hitler had declared his intention to rid Germany of all Jews. Many German Jews now started to flee abroad. Chagall was particularly shocked: he had witnessed the abhorrent effects of the anti-Semitic pogroms in Russia. He was also horrified at the Nazi campaign to shatter the world of modern art.

1937 Chagall is granted French citizenship. He is honored by having a room devoted to his work at the International Exhibition in Paris. Picasso paints *Guernica*, a response to the horrors of the Spanish Civil War (1936–9). German museums are forced to remove all of their works by Chagall under orders of the Nazi regime.
1938 Chagall has a one-man exhibition at the Palais des Beaux-Arts in Brussels. The assassination of a German diplomat in Paris by a Jew is used by the Nazis as a pretext to launch a violent anti-Jewish pogrom across Germany, called Kristallnacht.
1939 Vollard dies.

Hitler's Germany

Adolf Hitler (1889–1945) had come to power in Germany in 1933, promising to rescue the country from the humiliation it had suffered following World War I. He stirred up a frenzy of national pride by mobilizing the army, crushing opponents, and identifying minorities as enemies of Germany — notably the Jews. Ambitions to win back German territory lost in World War I created international tensions. By 1937, a new war looked inevitable.

▶ *Hitler turned Germany into an aggressive, militaristic nation with ambitions of world domination.*

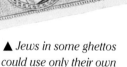

▲ *Jews in some ghettos could use only their own substandard currency.*

The Ghetto

When Chagall went to Poland in 1935, he visited Vilnius (now the capital of Lithuania) and Warsaw. He was shocked to see the conditions in which Jews were living. Treated worse than second-class citizens, they were confined to ghettos. It demonstrated to Chagall that the age-old anti-Jewish prejudices were not just a German phenomenon but were rife all over eastern Europe as well.

The Bible

Throughout the 1930s, Chagall continued to work on his set of etchings for Ambroise Vollard illustrating the Old Testament. As the threat to the Jews increased, the project gained in significance for him. By 1939, he had produced 66 of the 105 plates planned; they were etched and printed, and many were hand colored. But as the war loomed, Vollard died in a car crash. The project was not completed until the 1950s.

◀ Moses Breaking the Tablets of the Law *was one of the Bible plates completed in the 1930s.*

"Degenerate" Art

From the very beginning of Hitler's rule in Germany, the Nazi authorities waged war on modern art, and they took great delight in mocking it and destroying it. It was a crowd-pleasing policy, guaranteed to win approval from a public mystified by modern art. Jewish artists came in for particular scorn, and especially Chagall: three of his paintings were burned by the Nazis. In 1937, German museums were forced to submit their collections of modern art for ridicule at a huge *Exhibition of Degenerate Art (Entartete Kunst)* in Munich.

▲ *Chagall's* To My Wife *(1933) was featured in the Munich exhibition of 1937.*

▶ *A poster for an exhibition of "degenerate" art identifies the artists as Bolsheviks and Jews.*

◀ *Chagall painted* White Crucifixion *(1938) as the persecution of the Jews intensified.*

Making a Statement

As the 1930s drew on, Chagall painted fewer large canvases, concentrating on his prints and smaller works. An exception was his *White Crucifixion*, a work that reflects his growing anguish over the oppression of the Jews across Europe. In the background, Nazi soldiers attack a synagogue, and a village lies in flames before advancing soldiers bearing the red flag of Communism. The crucifixion was a theme that he had explored before: in 1912, he had painted a Cubist crucifixion scene called *Golgotha*. He saw in Christ, a Jew, a metaphor for Jewish suffering and a tragic point of impact between two religious cultures.

War and Escape

1939 As war threatens, the Chagalls move away from Paris to the Loire Valley.
1940 They move to Gordes in the south of France. In June, Germany invades northern France.
1941 Chagall and Bella leave for New York via Madrid and Lisbon; on the way, his paintings are impounded by the Spanish for five nerve-racking weeks. In New York, Chagall exhibits his paintings at the gallery of Pierre Matisse (1900–89), son of the great artist, who becomes Chagall's dealer.
1942 Chagall designs sets and costumes for Léonide Massine's ballet *Aleko*.

Following the German invasion of Poland in August 1939, Britain and France declared war on Germany. The following year, in June, the Germans invaded France and occupied the north, while southern France was ruled by the French Vichy government. Chagall was living in the South of France and still free to leave. Escape became urgent when, in 1941, the Vichy government introduced anti-Jewish policies. Assisted by an invitation from the Museum of Modern Art in New York, on June 23, Chagall and Bella arrived in the United States to begin a new life.

▼ *Arriving by ship in New York, Chagall saw the Statue of Liberty as a symbol of freedom and hope.*

Arriving in the United States

New York represented a new world for Chagall — a vertical city of skyscrapers, concrete, and glass, a vibrant cosmopolitan city swelled by thousands of new emigrants from Europe like himself. It was both exciting and alarming. Chagall was not happy to have been uprooted in this fashion and obstinately refused to learn English. He and Bella began to feel more settled when, after living in a series of hotels, they moved into an apartment on East 74th Street where Chagall could set up a studio.

◀ *In Nazi Europe, Jews had to wear a Star of David badge to signal their identity. "Jude" means Jew.*

Persecution of the Jews

Many hundreds of thousands of Jews fled from Germany and eastern Europe in the 1930s and during World War II. For those Jews who remained behind, the consequences were horrific. Massacres, famine, concentration camps, and gas chambers formed part of the German policy to annihilate the Jews. About seventy-five per cent of all European Jews died — more than six million people.

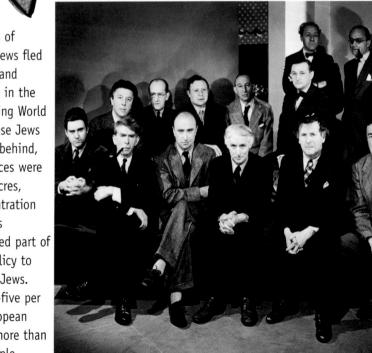

Artists in Exile

The huge number of gifted Europeans now living in the United States formed a vibrant expatriate community. They included the artists Fernand Léger, Georg Grosz, Max Ernst, Salvador Dali, and the Dutch abstract painter Piet Mondrian (1872–1944), the poet André Breton, the architect Ludwig Mies van der Rohe (1886-1969), and the Russian composer Igor Stravinsky (1882-1971).

◀ *At the* Artists in Exile *show at Pierre Matisse's gallery in 1942, Chagall is pictured seated, second from the right.*

◀ Chagall designed the costumes for Aleko, *a ballet based on "The Gypsies," a poem by the great Russian writer Aleksandr Pushkin (1799–1837).*

▶ Chagall's designs were used for the 1953 production of Aleko, *starring the Cuban ballerina Alicia Alonso (born 1921) and Igor Youskevitch (1912–94).*

Chagall and the Ballet

In 1942, Chagall was invited by the Russian Léonide Massine (1896–1979), a former dancer with the Ballets Russes, to design the sets and costumes for his new ballet *Aleko*, set to music by the Russian composer Peter Ilich Tchaikovsky (1840–93). When, because of union problems, the première was transferred to Mexico City, Chagall and Bella accompanied the troupe and worked together on the production. Reviving his talent for theatrical design learned in Moscow, Chagall helped make the event a critical triumph.

A Home Away from Home

In 1943, the Chagalls began to find refuge from New York in a rented house and studio at Cranberry Lake in the Adirondack Mountains. There they found peace and solace and could enjoy the landscape as they had in Europe. Chagall continued to paint wedding scenes, flowers, and circuses. All the while, he was haunted by the news from Europe — the ravages of the war in Russia, the destruction of Vitebsk, and the mounting evidence of the ghastly fate of the Jews. He showed his anguish in a number of paintings and drawings featuring crucifixions, blood-red colors, severed limbs, and distressed mothers with babies.

▶ The Juggler (1943) has echoes of the Cirque Vollard series. Painted in New York, it suggests the juggling that Chagall had to do to hold his life together.

Death and Theater

1944 Bella dies suddenly.

1945 World War II ends. Virginia Haggard McNeil becomes Chagall's housekeeper and lover. Chagall designs a production of Stravinsky's *The Firebird*.

1946 Chagall and Virginia move to the Catskill Mountains in New York State. The Museum of Modern Art in New York mounts a major retrospective of Chagall's work. Chagall spends three months in France. Virginia gives birth to their son David.

1947 Chagall returns to Paris to attend a large retrospective of his work, which marks the reopening of the Musée National d'Art Moderne. This is followed by retrospectives in Amsterdam, London, Zurich, and Berne.

During the summer of 1944, the Allied armies began to make real progress toward the defeat of Nazi Germany. Paris was liberated on August 25. But for Chagall, this news was overshadowed by deep personal tragedy: quite suddenly, Bella died. Chagall was devastated, but he was eventually coaxed out of depression by a new love. Following the end of the war, the world was shaken by the discovery of the true horror of the German concentration camps and the fate of the Jews in what became known as the Holocaust. In these years of recovery, the poetry, charm, and Jewishness of Chagall's work struck a chord, and he was honored by a series of major exhibitions in New York and Europe — all largely organized by his daughter Ida, who now acted as his business manager.

◄ *The Soviet army captured Berlin in April 1945, heralding the end of the war in Europe.*

Losing Bella

Chagall and Bella had spent an agreeable summer at Cranberry Lake when she fell ill with a viral infection. She was rushed to a hospital, but on September 22, she died. Chagall had lost his greatest soul mate and companion. They had been married for nearly thirty years and had been through the torment of two world wars together. She had been his inspiration and a trusted judge of his work. After her death, Chagall, now fifty-seven, was unable to work for nine months.

▶ Around Her *(1945) expresses the deep sense of loss and disorientation that Chagall felt after the death of his beloved wife Bella.*

Love For Life

From early 1946, Chagall and Virginia lived quietly in the beautiful Catskill Mountains in the north of New York State. This relationship restored his love for life and is reflected in his painting. Remembering a suggestion by Vollard, Chagall began to work on a series of joyful gouaches to illustrate *The Arabian Nights*. To convert these into printing plates, he used lithography — a process that was new to him but corresponded well to his painterly style.

The Firebird

One project that helped to restore Chagall to contentment was a commission, in the summer of 1945, to design the costumes and sets for a new production of *The Firebird* by Igor Stravinsky, the Russian composer now living in the United States. Stravinsky had provided the music for some of the most celebrated productions of the Ballets Russes in Paris in the years before World War I. These ballets were famous not only for their controversial music and supreme performances by leading Russian dancers but also for their striking costumes and sets. Chagall's designs followed in this tradition to great acclaim.

▲ *The happier mood of* The Flying Sleigh *(1945) marked the start of Chagall's recovery from the loss of Bella.*

▲ The Firebird *was first performed in Paris in 1910 with Tamara Platonovna Karsavina (1885–1978), one of the greatest dancers of the Ballet Russes, in the title role and costumes by Léon Bakst.*

Life With Virginia

Chagall's daughter Ida, who lived in New York, realized that her father needed help in his flat. She employed for him, as cook and housekeeper, a thirty-year-old English artist called Virginia Haggard McNeil. Chagall and Virginia became lovers, but because she was married, this relationship was kept secret. In June 1946, she gave birth to their son, David.

◄ *Chagall, photographed in 1951 with Virginia behind him, shows his delight when their son David picks up a paintbrush.*

The South of France

1948 Chagall leaves the United States for France. He meets the influential art dealer Aimé Maeght (1906–81), who becomes his representative in France. *Dead Souls* is finally published by Tériade (1897–1983), a Greek-born art critic and friend.
1951 Chagall travels to Israel for a series of retrospective exhibitions. Virginia leaves him.
1952 He marries Vava Brodsky. Chagall's daughter Ida remarries; her new husband is Franz Meyer, a Swiss gallery director. Both Ida and Franz subsequently play an important role in cataloging Chagall's achievement. Tériade publishes Chagall's etchings for La Fontaine's *Fables*.
1956 Tériade publishes Chagall's Bible etchings.

In 1948, Chagall returned with Virginia and David to live in France. This was not a final farewell to the United States. Chagall was deeply appreciative of what the United States had given him — a refuge, freedom, an appreciative art world, and devoted patrons. Chagall and Virginia first rented a large house at Orgeval, west of Paris. Then in 1950 — attracted, like Picasso and Matisse, to the warmth and sunlight of the Côte d'Azur in the southeastern corner of France — Chagall bought a large house called Les Collines ("The Hills") near Vence.

◀ *Picasso made his highly inventive pots, such his* Large Bird *(1953), in the south of France at a workshop at Vallauris, where Chagall also worked.*

Chagall Meets Vava

In France, Chagall and Virginia were drifting apart, and in 1951, Virginia left him, taking David with her. The following year, Chagall met Valentina (Vava) Brodsky at Tériade's house in the south of France. Of Jewish origin, born in Kiev, Ukraine, she had lived in Berlin during the Russian Revolution and spent the war in London. When they met, Chagall was immediately struck by her calm beauty. In July, Vava became his second wife. Chagall was sixty-five, and she was forty-seven. She remained his constant companion for the rest of his life, playing — as Bella had — a vital role as Chagall's inspiration and advisor.

▶ Portrait of Vava *(1953–6). Aside from his self-portraits, Chagall painted the portraits of his relatives, including Bella, Ida, and Vava.*

City of his Dreams

Chagall's new love for Vava coincided with a surge in his energy and productivity. Much of his painting of this era was inspired by Paris, where Vava had an apartment overlooking the Seine River. He claimed that he had dreamed of Paris when in America, and he was always delighted to return. In 1954, Aimé Maeght showed twenty-nine paintings created as a tribute to the city in his Parisian gallery.

▶ *In* Sunday *(1954), Chagall portrays Paris as a city of lovers, with a couple shining like the Sun over the Eiffel Tower, Notre Dame Cathedral, and the Seine River.*

Chagall in Vallauris

Like many twentieth-century artists before him, Chagall was intrigued by the possibilities of ceramics. He started to make pottery during a trip to Vence in 1949 and continued when he moved to the town the following year. From time to time, he met Picasso, with whom he had a friendly but prickly relationship. Picasso, and also Matisse, made pottery at the Madoura ceramics studio at Vallauris. Chagall followed suit, and over the next two decades, he created some 240 ceramic works — vases, plates, and tiles — all reflecting the recurring themes of his paintings.

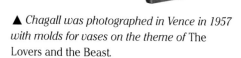

▲ *Chagall was photographed in Vence in 1957 with molds for vases on the theme of* The Lovers and the Beast.

Experiments with Stone

Also while living in Vence, in 1951, Chagall began making sculptures using marble or a soft limestone called Rogne stone. Most of these are small relief sculptures on blocks of stone cut to geometric shapes — like three-dimensional versions of his paintings. The key difference is an absence of color: Chagall depended entirely on the color of the stone and the shadows cast by his carving to achieve his subtle effects. He also had a few of his sculptures cast in bronze.

▶ *Chagall's sculpture* Moses *(1952–4), made of Rogne stone, shows a clear link to his Bible etchings.*

Theater and Stained Glass

1951 Matisse's chapel in Vence, decorated with stained glass, is consecrated.
1952 Chagall studies the stained-glass windows in Chartres Cathedral near Paris.
1957 He designs windows for a church at Assy, eastern France.
1958 He meets Charles Marq, director of the Simon Atelier in Reims, and begins work on his stained glass for the St. Etienne Cathedral in Metz.
1962 Chagall makes his third journey to Israel, for the inauguration of his stained-glass windows at the synagogue of the Medical Center of the Hadassah-Hebrew University, Jerusalem.
1964 He completes his ceiling painting at the Paris Opéra.

During the 1950s, Chagall was increasingly drawn to the idea of the artist as an all-around craftsman. He had demonstrated his versatility in his theater work, sculpture, and ceramics. Now he turned to stained glass, an art that was undergoing a revival. It suited his style perfectly: backlit by the sky, his bright and evocative colors became gemlike. With his Cubist background, he was also at ease with the fragmentation demanded by the structure of stained glass.

Stained Glass

◄ *In the United States, Chagall would have come across Art Nouveau lamps by Tiffany.*

Stained glass has been used since the Middle Ages to illustrate Bible stories and to turn the interiors of churches into magical light boxes. The colored and painted pieces of glass, held together with strips of lead, allowed great flexibility in design. Earlier in the twentieth century, this effect also appealed to decorative arts designers such as Louis Comfort Tiffany (1848–1933).

Daphnis and Chloë

In 1952, Chagall's publisher, Tériade, commissioned him to make a series of forty-two colored lithographs for the story of *Daphnis and Chloë*. He traveled with Vava to Greece to gain a feel for the authentic setting of this Greek myth. His lithographs were finally published in 1961. In 1958, he was asked to design the sets and costumes for the Paris Opéra production of the ballet *Daphnis and Chloë* by the French composer Maurice Ravel (1875–1937).

▶ Noon in Summer *(c. 1957–60). Chagall used gouache paintings to plan his lithographs for Daphnis and Chloë.*

▶ *For the windows of St. Etienne Cathedral in Metz, Chagall chose subjects from the Old Testament. Pictured here are* Jacob's Dream *and* Moses *(1960).*

Chagall's Windows

Chagall made stained glass for fifteen buildings. The first large commission came in 1958 from St. Etienne Cathedral in Metz. Produced in collaboration with the Simon Atelier in Reims, the windows were completed in 1968. Another major commission came in 1964, for a window called *The Kiss of Peace* for the United Nations Building in New York.

The Paris Opéra

In 1963, Chagall's old friend André Malraux, now Minister of Cultural Affairs, invited him to create a new ceiling for the nineteenth-century auditorium of Paris's famous opera house. This was not universally welcomed. Some voices in the French press questioned why one of France's great cultural monuments should be decorated by a Russian Jew. But Malraux stoutly defended his decision. It was a huge undertaking for Chagall, who was now seventy-six. The five segments of canvas covered a total area of about 722 square feet (220 square meters). They were painted on the ground in a studio before being transferred to the Opéra and raised to the ceiling. At the inauguration in 1964, Chagall declared the work his gift to the nation.

▲ The Paris Opéra ceiling, completed in 1964, features scenes inspired by Chagall's favorite operas and ballets.

Chagall Back in New York

In 1964, when Chagall and Vava visited New York for the unveiling of his United Nations window, the director of the New York Metropolitan Opera commissioned him to paint two huge murals to decorate the lobby of the opera company's new building. Called *The Sources of Music* and *The Triumph of Music*, they were completed in France in 1966 and installed so they can be seen from outside the building.

◄ Chagall puts the finishing touches to the assembled segments of the Opéra ceiling.

▲ The elaborate Paris Opéra is the best-known work of the architect Charles Garnier (1825–98). It was completed in 1875.

▼ The Metropolitan Opera House is part of the Lincoln Center, a cultural complex built in the 1960s.

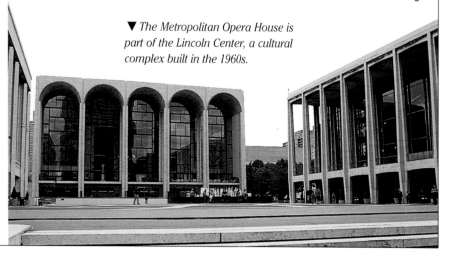

◄ Another pair of windows in St. Etienne Cathedral depicts *Original Sin* and The Expulsion from Paradise *(1963)*.

The Last Survivor

Chagall worked with frenetic energy to the end of his life. He continued painting with undiminished vigor, and he designed tapestries, stained-glass windows, and book illustrations. In 1965, when well into his seventies, he added to his range of skills when he designed a mosaic for the Fondation Maeght in St.-Paul-de-Vence. This work led to a series of designs for large-scale mosaics. He traveled to Israel, the United States, the Soviet Union, and Italy. Every year, he was honored with a major exhibition. By the end of his life, he had become the undisputed "grand old man" of twentieth-century art.

▲ Costume design for Pamina and Monostatos *(1922) by Leon Bakst. With* The Magic Flute, *Chagall again followed in the footsteps of Bakst, designing for the same opera.*

▶ *Round the Magic Flute (1965), one of Chagall's designs for the opera.*

Mozart's *The Magic Flute*

When the Metropolitan Opera in New York opened in 1967, one of the first productions was *The Magic Flute* by Wolfgang Amadeus Mozart (1756–91). The sets and costumes had been commissioned from Chagall two years before while he was working on the lobby paintings. The sets were designed in Vence and built in New York, and Chagall traveled there to make the final adjustments. The effect was, as usual, richly colorful and busy — too busy for some critics, who complained that Chagall's designs distracted the eye from the performances.

National Honors

On January 1, 1977, Chagall was awarded the Grand Cross of the Legion of Honor, France's highest decoration. Later that year, in October, he became the first living artist to be given an exhibition at the Louvre, France's most prestigious museum. It was opened by the president of France. In Israel, Chagall was considered to be the greatest living Jewish artist. In that same year, he traveled to Jerusalem for a ceremony in his honor.

The Last of the Innovators

Chagall had outlived Matisse and Léger — both near neighbors in the South of France — by some thirty years. Picasso died in 1973, André Malraux in 1976. In his nineties, Chagall was recognized as the last of the great innovators of early twentieth-century art, the last survivor of the artists who had lived through all the great art movements — Fauvism, Cubism, Futurism, Surrealism, Expressionism — and known many of the participants.

Last Years in St.-Paul-de-Vence

By the time Chagall moved to the village of St.-Paul-de-Vence, it had become a famous meeting place for artists. Its hotel-restaurant La Colombe d'Or was decorated with paintings by famous artists who had eaten or stayed there, including Picasso, Braque, Léger, and Chagall. Just outside the village lay the prestigious Fondation Maeght with its priceless collection of twentieth-century art and its succession of notable exhibitions. It was a fitting place for Chagall to end his days.

▲ The Prophet Isaiah *(1968) was one of the large canvases that Chagall painted for his* Biblical Message *series.*

◀ *St.-Paul-de-Vence is a pretty hilltop village of medieval origin in the hills above Nice. It is celebrated for its connections with twentieth-century art.*

Chagall's Legacy

Chagall was widely admired and loved for his highly personal, poetic vision of the world. After World War II, changing trends had given prominence to various art movements utterly different and alien to Chagall's work, such as Abstract Expressionism, Pop Art, and Minimalism. Despite these changes, Chagall remained one of the most popular artists of the twentieth century — in itself, a remarkable achievement. Critics were often disdainful, but Chagall always had support from the public.

Marc ChAgALL

◄ *Chagall signed his name at the foot of all his paintings, usually with "Marc Chagall," or "Chagall Marc," with the "Marc" sometimes floating off the line as if detached.*

Vitebsk Remembers Chagall

In Vitebsk, Chagall has not always been considered a cherished son. To be fair, this feeling was mutual. Chagall himself was sometimes dismissive of his home town, suggesting that it was small-minded and provincial: "a strange town, an unhappy town, a boring town," he wrote in *My Life*. He always resented the way in which he had been ejected from the art academy that he founded there. In 1973, on his return to the Soviet Union, he refused even to go to Vitebsk. In 1991, however, a modest Chagall Art Center was set up in Vitebsk, and a statue of Chagall with a floating Bella was erected to his memory. His home has been restored and turned into a museum decorated with copies of his early paintings.

▶ *This photo of Chagall was taken on July 6, 1984, the day before his ninety-seventh — and last — birthday.*

The Chagall Museum

From 1955 on, Chagall worked on a series of seventeen massive canvases intended for a chapel in Vence. He called the paintings *The Biblical Message* (see page 43). In the end, he donated them to the nation, and they formed the basis — along with some 450 other works — of the Musée National Message Biblique Marc Chagall (or Chagall Museum).

▲ *The Chagall Museum in Nice was opened by André Malraux in 1973.*

International Recognition

Chagall achieved international fame during his own lifetime. He received countless honors, such as the European Erasmus Prize and honorary doctorates from Glasgow University, Brandeis University in Massachusetts, and Notre Dame in Indiana. His work was widely collected by museums and galleries around the world and became well known through prints and reproductions. Because Chagall's imagery and themes remained fairly constant throughout his career and his style remained relatively consistent, his work is instantly recognizable.

Chagall's Artistic Contribution

The world of Chagall is unique. The flying lovers, the lone violinist, the hints of Russia, the farm animals, and upside-down heads all create a richly imagined interior vision. This imagery, and the intensity of his colors, have become so familiar that it is hard to recall just how original — shocking even — Chagall's work seemed in the early decades of the twentieth century. Chagall painted as if he had an image that he needed urgently to transmit, and he was not going to allow the constraints of formal academic skills stand in the way. He had always resisted the stifling conformity of the art schools. "I like drawing badly," he once claimed. Through his spontaneity and his uncompromising will to paint in the way he chose, Chagall helped liberate art from the constraints of the past.

▼ Birthday *(1915) dates from the year of Chagall's marriage to Bella. The lovers float into the air with elation in a room that pays scant heed to perspective.*

▲ *A light ripple of humor runs through much of Chagall's work, as seen in this self-portrait in ink and pastel called* The Artist *(1959).*

Glossary

abstract A style of art that does not represent objects as they appear in reality but reduces and simplifies forms and objects. Abstract art abandons the principle that art must imitate nature.

anti-Semitism Prejudice and discrimination against Jews as a religious, ethnic, or racial group.

atelier French word meaning studio or workshop.

Art Nouveau An ornamental style of European and U.S. art that lasted from 1890 to 1910, characterized by the use of long, curving lines based on plant forms. This so-called "new" style (the word nouveau means "new" in French) was applied primarily to architecture, interior design, jewelry, glass design, and illustration.

avant-garde A term used to refer to persons or actions that are different or experimental, particularly with respect to the arts.

Bolshevik A Russian term, meaning "one of the majority," used to describe a member of the Russian Social Democratic Workers' Party led by Vladimir Ilich Lenin (1870–1924).

collage A picture made by sticking together bits of paper or other materials.

Communism A political system that favors a classless society and collective ownership of goods and services.

composition The arrangement of the parts of something. The term is used to refer to the way in which objects are arranged, usually in a painting or sculpture.

Constructivism A Russian abstract art movement invented in about 1913 by Vladimir Tatlin (1885–1953) in which works of art are "constructed" from a variety of materials, such as sheet metal, wire, plastic, and glass. Constructivism, which was inspired by modern machinery and technology, was later applied to architecture.

Cubism An art movement of the early twentieth century that aimed to represent three dimensions on a two-dimensional plane. Cubist artists represented objects from more than one angle so that several different aspects of the subject could be seen at one time.

Dadaism An anti-art movement started in 1915 that attempted to express the confusion and disorder of the world after World War I by rejecting traditional culture and ideas of beauty in art.

drypoint A method of engraving in which a needle or sharp tool is used directly on the surface of a metal plate to create a design without the use of acid. The burr created by the carving of the metal surface with the tool produces particular effects in the finished product. Drypoint is often used to make additions to an etching.

engraving The process of carving a design into a block of wood or plate of metal, or the prints taken from this process.

etching A method of engraving in which a design is burned onto a metal plate using acid, or the print taken from the process.

expressionism A movement in modern art that broke away from naturalism and distorted or exaggerated reality for emotional effect.

Fauvism An early twentieth-century art movement led in part by the French painter Henri Matisse (1869–1954), who used vivid colors, flat patterns, and distorted forms. The word fauve means "wild beast" in French.

folk art A term used to describe traditional objects made by people with no formal artistic training.

folklore Legends, beliefs, customs, and art forms of a group of people that have been passed down from generation to generation.

Futurism A politically driven art movement that began in Italy in 1909. It glorified the modern world of machinery, speed, and violence.

ghetto A restricted area of a city where members of a minority live.

gouache Opaque watercolor paint.

Holocaust The Nazi extermination of millions of Jews during World War II.

Impressionism A nineteenth-century art movement that took a more spontaneous approach to painting, attempting to capture and portray the atmosphere of a given moment, usually identified by a strong concern for the changing qualities of light.

lithograph A print made by pressing paper onto a stone that has been engraved and treated with chemicals and water.

manifesto A public statement made by a person or group, outlining their actions and intentions.

Menshevik A Russian term, meaning "one of the minority," used to describe a member of the non-Leninist faction of the Russian Social Democratic Workers' Party, led by L. Martov (1873–1923).

Nazism The National Socialist regime of Hitler's Germany (1933 to 1945); the political beliefs and methods of Hitler's party.

Old Master An artist of an earlier period, usually from the fifteenth to the eighteenth centuries, of noteworthy skill.

Orphism A term invented by Guillaume Apollinaire (1880–1918) in 1913 to describe an nonobjective art movement in French painting in which color, not form, was the principal element in artistic expression. Followers of this movement sought to create a connection between abstract forms and music.

patron A person who gives money to a person or group to perform a certain task or for some other worthy purpose. Patrons sometimes support artists and writers.

pogrom An organized riot and massacre of helpless people.

Postimpressionism A term applied to an art movement of the late nineteenth and early twentieth centuries whose style developed out of or in reaction against that of the Impressionists.

retrospective exhibition An exhibition showing the work of a particular artist dating from the beginning to the end of his or her career.

Suprematism An abstract art movement invented in 1915 by the Russian painter Kasimir Malevich (1878–1935) that uses basic geometric shapes and limited colors.

Surrealism An aesthetic movement of the 1920s and 1930s that attempted to portray thought, dreams, and the imagination.

Index

Index